This Annual
belongs to:

....

DohVinci

Contents

6   Be a True Artist
8   Styler Success
10   Drawing Styles
12   Crank Up the Colour
13   Colour Twist
14   Spring Style
16   New View
17   One-of-a-kind suprise
18   Artify Easter
20   3D Messages
22   Easy Envelopes
23   Face Time
24   Little & Large
26   Summer Love
28   Sweet Tree
30   Life's a Party
32   Beautiful Balance
34   Sunny Side Up
35   Magic Moments
36   Word Art
38   Falling into Autumn
40   Creative Upcycle
42   Signature Style
43   Cool Culture
44   Trick or Treat?
46   Spooky Jack
47   Doodle Art
48   Cool Wonderland
50   Style Your Season
52   Wrapped with Art
54   Capture the World
56   Snow Friend
57   Mirror Me
58   School Swag
60   Amazing Makes
61   Art-tastic Wish List

Published 2015. Pedigree Books Limited, Beech Hill House, Walnut Gardens, Exeter, Devon EX4 4DH. www.pedigreebooks.com – books@pedigreegroup.co.uk
The Pedigree trademark, email and website addresses, are the sole and exclusive properties of Pedigree Group Limited, used under licence in this publication.

Be a True Artist

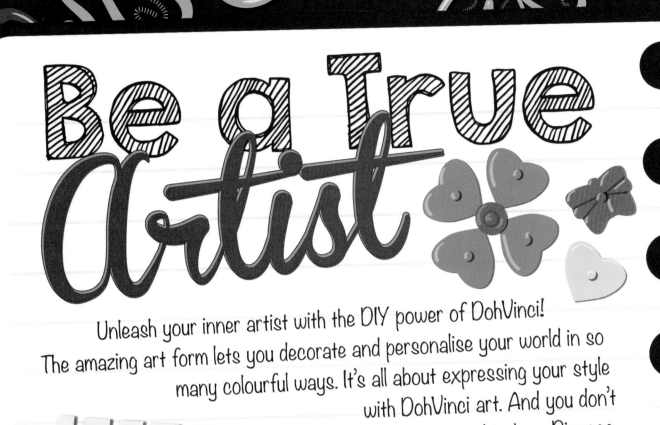

Unleash your inner artist with the DIY power of DohVinci!
The amazing art form lets you decorate and personalise your world in so
many colourful ways. It's all about expressing your style
with DohVinci art. And you don't
need to be a Picasso
to make creations that
pop. Inside this Annual
you'll find lots of easy
projects to make with
relatively little mess.

You can use the DohVinci Styler to design on
many different surfaces. Ask a parent before
decorating a household item as the compound
can stain some surfaces.

Permanent:
- Unfinished wood
- Paper mache
- Ceramic
- Cardboard
- Paper
- Craft pumpkins

Semi-permanent:
- Glass
- Canvas
- Painted metal
- Duct tape

If you make a mistake, all you have
to do is wipe it off and begin again.

Once you are done designing,
let it firm up for a one-of-a-kind
creation you can keep and show off!

Time to make your mark and show everybody who you are!

Styler Success

Are you ready to create bold art and experience your imagination in 3D? Bring your DohVinci Styler and Deco Pop colour tubes to a table and release the ultimate tools of creativity! Decide what to enhance with the DohVinci design compound and follow these steps for Styler success.

Deluxe Styler

Decorating with the DohVinci Styler is as easy as 1, 2, 3!

1. Choose a colour tube.
2. Pop it into the Styler.
3. Aim, squeeze, design!

Top tips for best results:

- Keep your design flat.
- Move the Styler slowly and towards your body.
- Hold the Styler at an angle, similar to how you hold a pencil.
- While you're squeezing, make sure the Styler tip touches the surface of your project.
- Don't forget to put the colour cap back on the compound capsule when you're done.
- Always handle your creations with care.

If the colour isn't sticking, press the Styler tip against the surface. Make a dot and then release the Styler.

When you want to change colours, push the tube backward out of the Styler, pop in a new one and keep designing.

If you're finding it hard to squeeze, flip the Styler upside down to change your grip.

If you have a Deluxe Styler, you can experiment with several amazing tip nozzles to create different art effects. You can use the tip as a stamp as well!

You can use the DohVinci compound like glue, too. Squeeze a dot onto the back of an embellishment and press it onto your design.

Holding your Styler:

Drawing Styles

There are a bunch of cool ways to use the Styler tool to create personal designs. The pattern potential is endless! Different ways to design with the Styler are shown here. Practise the easier strokes on the left page before going on to master the more advanced DohVinci skills on the right page.

Lines

Squeeze and move slowly across a surface.

Lot 'o Dots

Make a quick squeeze against the surface. Press in slightly at the end for a clean finish.

Zigger Zagger

Direct the Styler side to side in short motions, moving it down the surface toward you.

Chevron

Draw wide zig-zag lines in rows, making each row a different colour.

Waves

With one continuous squeeze, make a line of semicircles in a row.

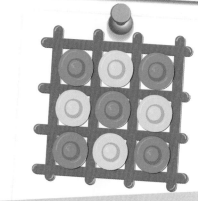

Tic Tac Dot

Create criss-crossed lines using the Styler, then switch colours and fill in the holes with dots.

DohVinci

Move the Styler around in a circular motion, from the outside in. Raise the Styler as you move to create a 3D effect.

Spectacular Spiral

With one long squeeze, move the Styler back and forth in loops, touching the sides of the loops as you go. Change colours and use the Lot o' Dots technique to add spots to the middle of the loops.

There are no limits to what you can achieve. Use your imagination to create your own DohVinci style and 3D details.

Crazy 8 Braid

Snake It

Make several figures of 8 back and forth without breaking a squeeze.

Handle completed design with care. The compound designed to firm up over time, but firmness will vary by thickness of application and environmental factors, including humidity.

If you don't love what you did and need a do-over, simply wipe it away and start again. Once you are happy with your art, let it firm up for a beautiful, keepable or even giftable creation!

Crank Up the Colour

Do you love crazy colours that clash or cute colours that connect? Use this colour wheel to help you pick your next Deco Pop tube for DohVinci delights!

Harmonise: close colours.

Warm colours have red tones, like 'Wink at Me Pink' and 'Pop of Purple.'

Contrast: opposite colours.

Complement: colours to the left and right.

Cool colours have blue tones, like 'You Blue My Mind' and 'Get Real Teal.'

Colour Twist

Can't pick between 'Red-iculous' or 'Lazy Daisy' yellow? Don't think there is a perfect single colour to make your project POP? Mix your own colours for a truly unique design.

1. Set up the DohVinci Colour Mixer. Place an empty Deco Pop tube into the centre of the wheel. Press down with the plunger to remove the plug.

2. Now place the empty tube into the base.

3. Load full Deco Pop tubes into the wheel. Twist the wheel to select your colour, positioning the full tube over the top of the empty one.

4. Use the plunger to press out your colour choice. Squeeze two or more colours into the tube.

5. Replace the bottom of the tube and load it into the Styler.

6. Aim, squeeze and design wild 3D lines in a cascade of colour!

Think of arty names for your new colour combos!

Spring Style

Colour in this fresh pattern with pens or pencils and be inspired for your next DohVinci design.

New View

The only thing better than having your own space is making it one-of-a-kind, like you. Your bedroom window is like a blank canvas, waiting for you to transform it with DohVinci art!

Draw the world as you would love to see it.

Window Art

How to make:

1. Check with your parents if it is OK to design on your window.

2. Make sure the glass is clean and dry.

3. Load a Deco Pop tube into the Styler and dream up a colourful picture.

4. First, try drawing blooming flowers.

5. Next try creating floating hearts, popping fireworks or frozen snowflakes.

6. Another idea is making a silly face or glasses on a mirror and standing in front of it for a funny photo!

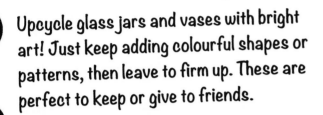

One-of-a-kind Surprise

Upcycle glass jars and vases with bright art! Just keep adding colourful shapes or patterns, then leave to firm up. These are perfect to keep or give to friends.

Fab flower holder

How to make:

1. Check with your parents if it is OK to design on a glass vase.

2. Make sure the glass is clean and dry.

3. Load a Deco Pop tube into the Styler and dream up a colourful picture.

4. First, try drawing blooming flowers.

5. Next try creating floating hearts, popping fireworks or frozen snowflakes.

Glass is a great surface to practise on because it is a semi-permanent surface for DohVinci. Your 3D art will stick very well, but once firm it can come off when forcibly removed.

DohVinci may fade in UV light over time.

Artify Easter

The hunt for the best DIY Easter decorations is over. Be inspired by the fresh and fun ideas here and amp up the awesome spring holiday. Once you are happy with your art, simply set it aside to firm up.

Adorable eggs

How to make:

1. Use the egg box to hold an egg while you use the DohVinci Styler to decorate it.

2. First, design colourful patterns.

3. Press craft gems onto your design for extra flair.

4. Create egg creatures by drawing a face.

5. Press on googly eyes to finish.

6. There are tons of ways to decorate your eggs – check out these super-bright shells.

You will need:

- Paper mache eggs
- Old egg box
- DohVinci Styler and Deco Pop tubes
- Craft gems
- Googly eyes

Beautiful basket

You will need:

- Cardboard basket
- DohVinci Styler and Deco Pop tubes
- Foam stickers and craft gems
- Paper or plastic grass

How to make:

1. Use the Styler to make a special design on the sides and handle of the basket to show what Easter means to you.

2. Enhance the 3D look with foam stickers and gems – it's easy to simply press them directly onto the compound.

3. Fill the basket with grass and add your eggs and flowers. When you are done, display your art in your room or share it with your family.

Brilliant blooms

You will need:

- Old egg box
- Scissors
- DohVinci Styler and Deco Pop tubes
- Craft gems and badges

How to make:

1. Cut the egg box into individual cups.

2. Cut the edges of each cup into petals. Experiment with different shapes, sizes and styles for the petals.

3. Decorate the blooms with bursts of colour. Use the Styler to layer the design compound for a cool look. Play around with exciting patterns.

4. Press on gems, badges or other decorations. Let your imagination shine!

3D Messages

Try creating some fabulous 3D cards for your family and friends!

Made with love

You will need:

- Templates from page 21
- Tracing paper, pencil, coloured paper (optional)
- A4 card sheets
- Scissors
- Glue stick
- DohVinci Styler and Deco Pop tubes

How to make:

1. Cut out a template on the opposite page, or use tracing paper to copy the designs onto coloured paper.

2. Fold a piece of A4 card in half and cut along the fold line. Fold each piece in half to make a greeting card.

3. Stick the template onto the front of the card.

4. Decorate the card with an extra special DohVinci design and leave it to one side to firm up.

5. Write your special message and give the card to a friend.

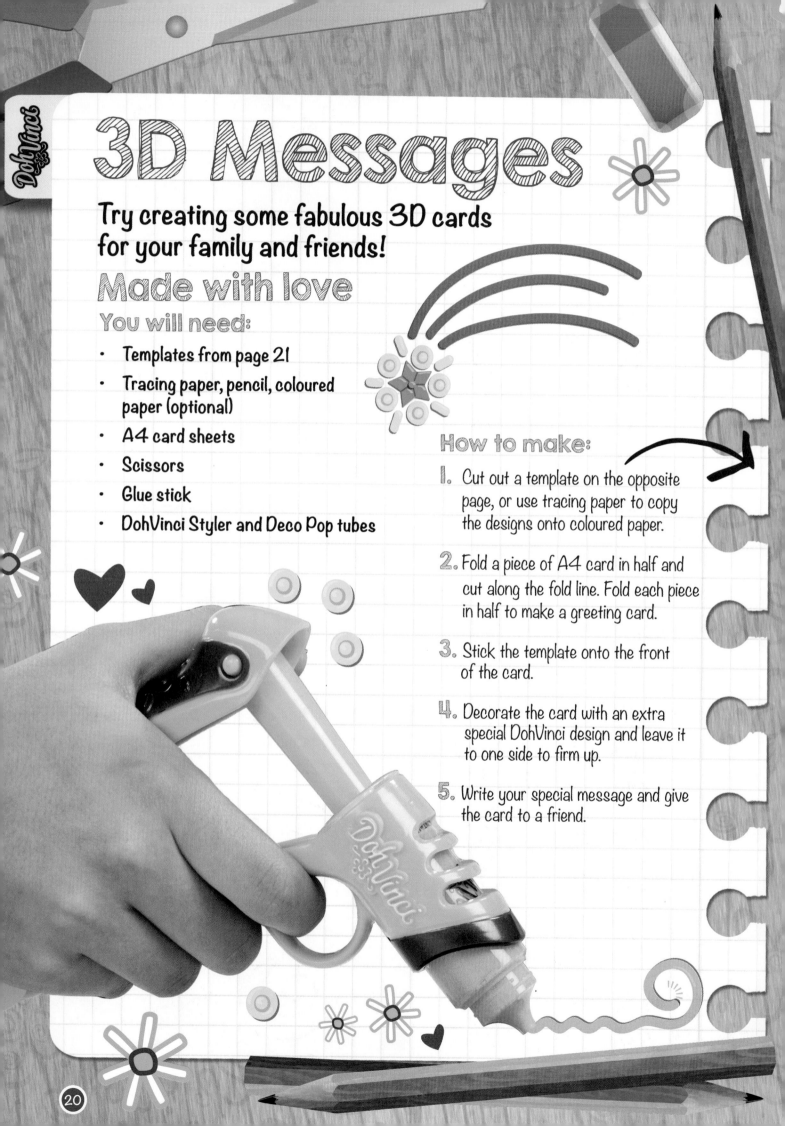

Happy Birthday!

Happy Mother's Day

Get Well Soon

Happy Easter!

Easy Envelopes

You can make all your letters and cards personal by decorating paper and envelopes with DohVinci designs! Boost your messages with unique DohVinci art and give them to the people you love the most.

You will need:
- Colour paper
- Pen
- Envelope
- Stickers
- DohVinci Styler and Deco Pop tubes

How to make:

1. Write a letter to an artist pen pal and use your signature style to make a small design by your name. Set aside to firm up.

2. Slide the card or letter into an envelope and seal it with a sticker.

3. Design a fab decoration and colour co-ordinate for the season. Allow the art to firm up before giving the letter to your friend.

Face Time

The more you draw, the better your art will become. Photocopy, scan or cut out this page from the Annual and use your Styler to bring the bunny to life in dazzling 3D.

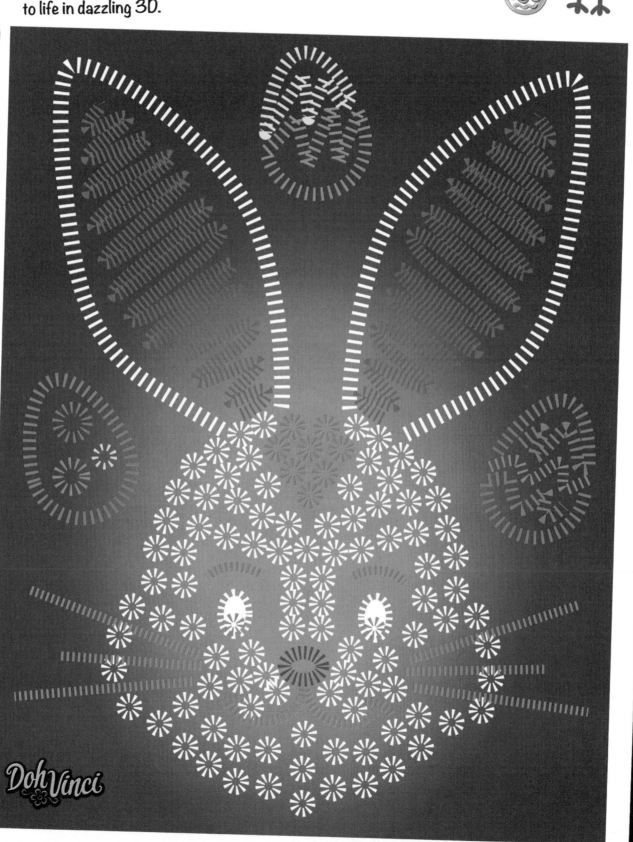

DohVinci

DohVinci

Little & Large

Practise drawing to improve your DohVinci design technique! Use the grid lines to copy the small picture into the big box, then colourise your art.

"Learn the rules like a pro, So you can break them like an artist."
Pablo Picasso - artist (1881-1973)

Use this technique to sketch a design on paper and then transfer it to canvas.

Summer Love

Colour in this summer pattern with pens or pencils and get ready for your next DohVinci project.

Sweet Tree

A sweet friend deserves this fun lollipop tree! It's likely that you have some spare pots at home – just ask an adult to show you the ones you can upcycle.

Aim, squeeze, DESIGN!

You will need:
- Clay flower pot
- Pencil
- Styrofoam ball
- Lollipop sweets
- DohVinci Styler and Deco Pop tubes

How to make:

1. Use a pencil to draw a cute flower design on the outside of the pot.

2. Decorate the pot with your DohVinci Styler and Deco Pop colour tubes.

3. Place the foam ball in the pot.

4. Poke the lollipops into the ball, keeping them close together. Fill the foam with lollipop sweeties! Set aside the pot so the compound becomes firm.

There are unlimited ways to fill pots with DohVinci art. Let your imagination grow and flower!

DohVinci

1

2

3

Don't worry if you aren't keen on your design. Simply wipe away and start again.

4

Life's a Party!

Life's a party! Make your next party magical with some fabulous masquerade masks! Invite your besties to turn up the volume and create their own mask art, then play some carnival games!

You will need:

Tracing paper
Pencil
Card
Scissors
DohVinci Styler and
Deco Pop tubes
Craft glue
Paper straws or wooden
craft dowels

How to make:

1. Use some tracing paper and the pencil to draw over a mask template on the opposite page.

2. Copy the tracing onto card and cut it out. Cut out the eyeholes.

3. Customise the mask with carnival colours and leave it to firm up.

4. Turn the mask over and use the glue to stick a straw or dowel in the centre. Once the glue is dry, use the stick to hold the mask to your face. Get ready to wear and share!

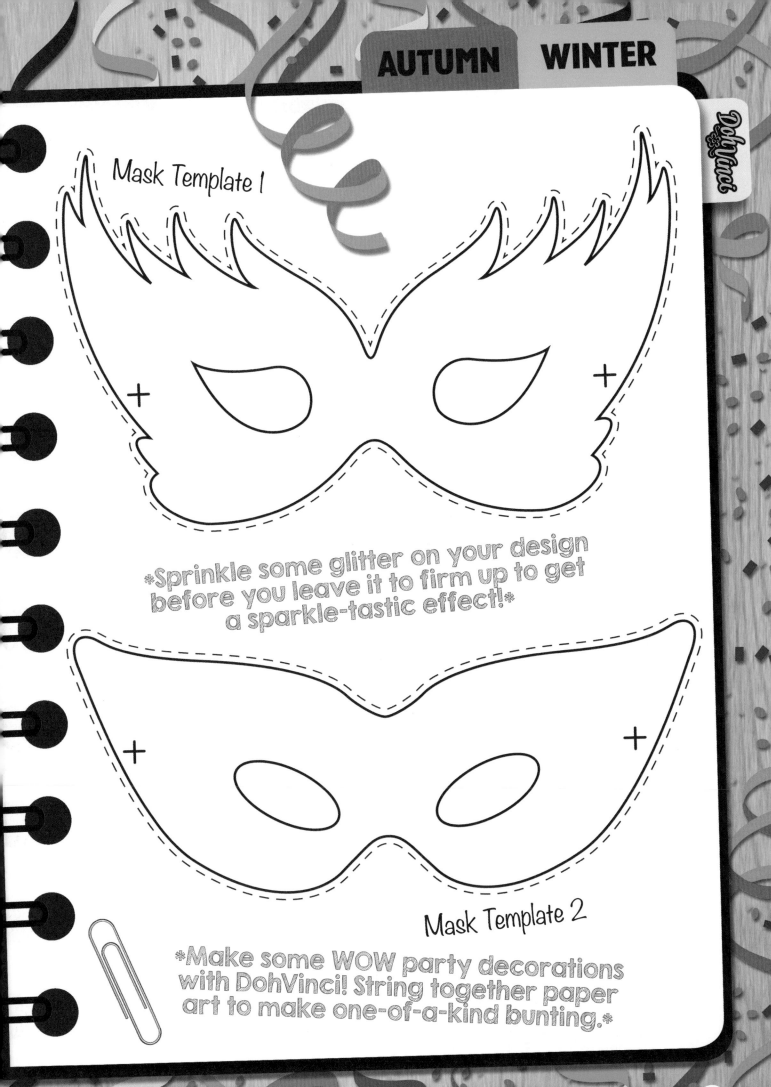

Mask Template 1

Sprinkle some glitter on your design before you leave it to firm up to get a sparkle-tastic effect!

Mask Template 2

Make some WOW party decorations with DohVinci! String together paper art to make one-of-a-kind bunting.

DohVinci

Beautiful Balance

Drawing symmetrical designs can be so pleasing! Something is symmetrical when it is exactly the same on both sides. A central dividing line (a mirror line) can be drawn on it to show where the two sides meet. Complete the symmetry on these pages.

Make symmetrical art on your next DohVinci creation! Why don't you experiment on a wooden photo frame or keepsake box? If you make a mistake, it's easy to wipe the art away and draw again.

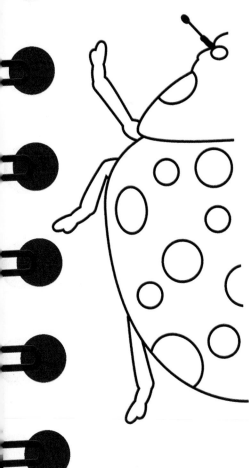

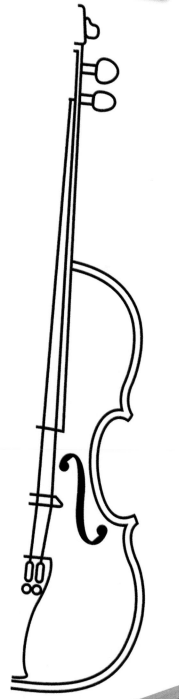

"I found I could say things with colour and shapes that I couldn't say any other way."
Georgia O'Keeffe - artist
(1887-1986)

Sunny Side Up

DohVinci

What's your favourite seaside memory?
Draw your memories in 3D with DohVinci! Photocopy,
scan or cut out this page from the Annual and use your
Styler to fill it with sunshine and sand.

Magic Moments

Best frame ever!

Celebrate your favourite photos by keeping them in special frames. Show the world your artistic flair and display your style for everyone to see! If you want to start afresh, remove the DohVinci compound before it firms up and squeeze again.

You will need: Unfinished wooden photo frame, DohVinci Styler and Deco Pop tubes, photo, sticky tape

How to make:

1. Lay the frame flat on a table.
2. Using your fave colours, enhance the border with DohVinci doodles and patterns, working in lines from the inside edge to the outside.
3. Keep the design symmetrical and make hearts the main theme. Use these pictures as inspiration, but feel free to design your own way.
4. Handle your design with care as you stick the photo behind the frame.
5. Set aside the art to firm up and admire the feast of colours you have created!

35

Word Art

Stuck behind a creative block? Kickstart your imagination by drawing art inspired by these words. Exercising your mind muscles will help you go the extra mile with your next DohVinci decorations!

Sea creature

Love

Space friend

Jungle tree

Be inspired by famous, great artists and trace a landscape scene on a large piece of paper.

Fantasy pet

Woodland elf

"I dream of painting and then I paint my dream."
Vincent van Gogh - artist (1853-1890)

Falling into Autumn

Colour in this autumnal pattern with pens or pencils and dream up new DohVinci decorations!

DohVinci

Creative Upcycle

Creating art with already used things can often make you feel happier than starting from scratch. Spark your imagination and use your DohVinci Styler to explore your creativity! If you want to start again, simply scrape away the compound before it firms up and carry on squeezing.

Get crafty! Test your DohVinci skills with an upcycling challenge! See what you can save from around your home and transform it into smart art. Just remember to ask an adult before you begin.

Dressing table tidy

You will need:

Empty tissue box, scissors, DohVinci Styler and Deco Pop tubes

How to make:

1. Give the empty tissue box a facelift by cutting off the top.
2. Deck out the box with a zesty design and leave it to firm up.
3. Now you have a super-cute place to store your beauty accessories on your dressing table.

Scale up!

Once you have mastered a smaller box, try upcycling a shoebox to keep your treasures safe.

Posy bottle

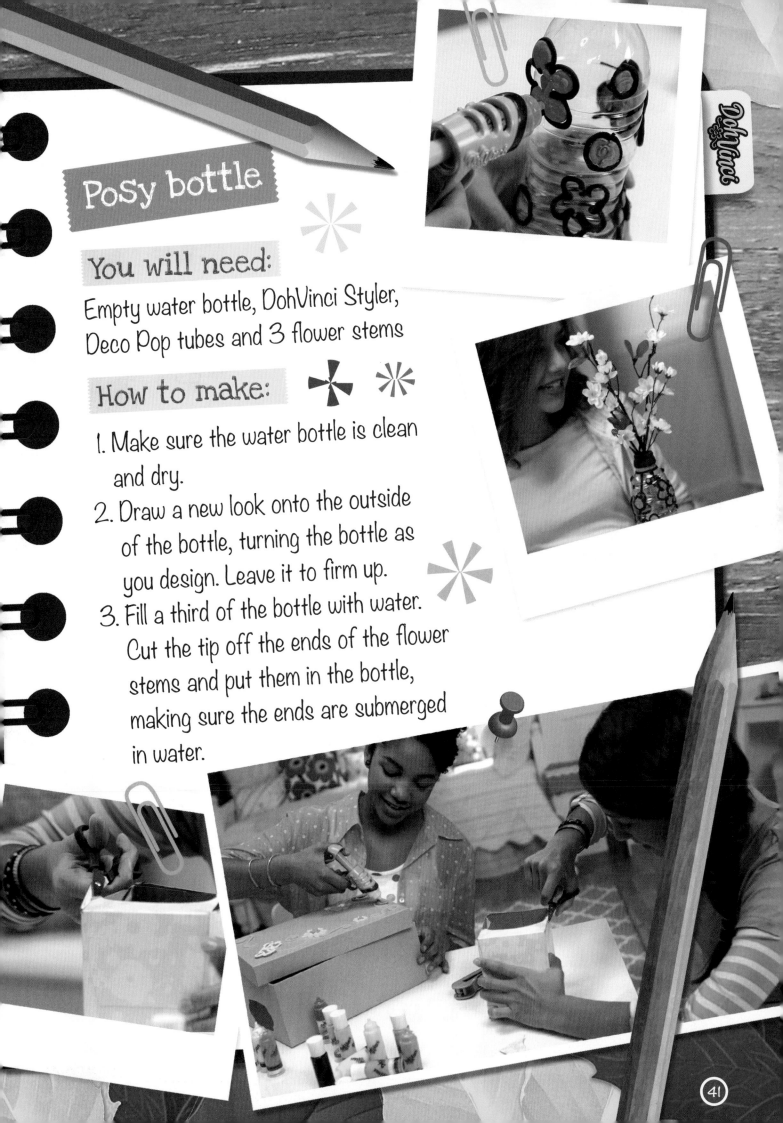

You will need:

Empty water bottle, DohVinci Styler, Deco Pop tubes and 3 flower stems

How to make:

1. Make sure the water bottle is clean and dry.
2. Draw a new look onto the outside of the bottle, turning the bottle as you design. Leave it to firm up.
3. Fill a third of the bottle with water. Cut the tip off the ends of the flower stems and put them in the bottle, making sure the ends are submerged in water.

Signature STYLE

Grab your own monogram letter from a craft store and cover it with DohVinci 3D creativity! Then make similar surprise gifts for your artsy friends. These giant letters look SO pop-tastic on a wall or shelf. Stand out and be different!

You will need:

Large craft letter
DohVinci Styler
and Deco Pop tubes

How to make:

1. Gather your fave Deco Pop colour tubes.
2. Use the Styler to squeeze a delicious-looking design on top of the letter. Layer different colours of the compound to make a high impact. Choose colours that reflect your personality.
3. Leave the art to firm up, turn the letter on its side and decorate the edge.
4. Repeat step 3 until all the edges have been dressed with colour.

Cool Culture

Check out this cool Calavera design! A brightly decorated skull motif is often made by people who celebrate the 'Day of the Dead' holiday in Mexico. Photocopy, scan or cut out this page from the Annual and use your Styler to make a unique impression.

Trick or Treat?

Everyone loves to decorate a pumpkin for the Halloween holiday. DohVinci takes away all the mess of carving a pumpkin - you can design straight onto it! Keep your creepy 3D creature forever to freak out your friends....

You will need: Craft pumpkin, Pencil, DohVinci Styler, Deco Pop tubes and Fairy lights

How to make:

1. Take your time to sketch a Halloween face or spooky pattern on the pumpkin.

2. Load a Deco Pop tube into the Styler and trace the design with DohVinci compound. Choose eerie colours or crazy combinations so they pop off the orange background. Allow the design to firm up.

3. Wind fairy lights around the pumpkin, turn them on and prepare to gasp at the glowing lantern.

Spookify a Halloween party with playful window art! How about a spider in its web, a pumpkin or a ghost? You can decorate nearly anything, from a balloon to a craft skull!

Spooky Jack

DohVinci

Practise your DohVinci skills on this classic Halloween design and pin it up for a party. Photocopy, scan or cut out this page from the Annual and use your Styler to add devilish colours.

AUTUMN

DohVinci

Doodle Art

"I paint because I need to." Frida Kahlo - artist (1907-1954)

Unleash your freestyle drawing skills! Use your favourite pencils to finish this awesome Autumn scene.

Cool Wonderland

Colour in this frosty pattern with pens or pencils and get ready for more DohVinci art.

Style Your Season

Make Christmas extra special by celebrating your creativity in wonderful 3D! Deck crafty decorations with holiday colours, then gift wrap them for your best friends or keep for your family to admire.

Lovely lanterns

You will need:

- Empty mason jars
- DohVinci Styler and Deco Pop tubes
- White craft sand/white glitter
- Battery tealight candles

How to make:

1. Make sure the mason jars are empty, clean and dry.

2. Put a Deco Pop tube in the Styler and decorate the jars with merry designs inspired by the holiday. How about holly leaves or stars? Set the jars aside until the compound firms up.

3. Pour some craft sand into each jar to look like snow.

4. Turn on the battery candles and place them in the jars.

Snowflake ornaments

You will need:

- Lolly sticks
- PVA glue and brush
- DohVinci Styler and Deco Pop tubes
- Ribbon

How to make:

1. Layer three or more lolly sticks to make a star shape.

2. Glue the sticks together where they overlap.

3. Load a Deco Pop tube into your Styler and decorate the snowflake frame. Put it to one side to firm up.

4. Loop a length of ribbon and tie the ends. Glue the knot to the back of the snowflake. Repeat the steps to make many colourful snowflakes!

Rockin' paper chains

You will need:

- A4 paper (different colours)
- Scissors
- DohVinci Styler and Deco Pop tubes
- Glue stick

How to make:

1. Fold a piece of paper in half and then in half again. Unfold the paper and cut along the fold lines so you have strips of paper which are all the same size.

2. Pop a Deco Pop tube into your Styler and draw totally original designs along the strips of paper, leaving the top and bottom ends empty. Wait for the art to firm up.

3. To start the chain, run a glue stick along the ends of a finished strip. Create a loop with the art facing outward and press the ends together.

4. Carry on the chain by putting one end of another strip through the first loop. Paste glue on the ends of the second strip and make a circle that links the two strips together. Carry on the chain!

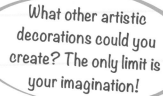

What other artistic decorations could you create? The only limit is your imagination!

Wrapped with Art

DohVinci

There's nothing better than giving the gift of art, and your DohVinci Styler is the key to making way-cool gifts. You can make a box that's as unique as the gift inside! If you want to change anything as you design, just wipe away before it firms up and draw again.

One-of-a-kind box

You will need:
DohVinci Styler and Deco Pop tubes
Plain box

How to make:

1. Prepare the Styler by popping in a Deco Pop colour.

2. Imagine a design that fits with the gift inside the box and make your art ideas become reality with the DohVinci compound.

3. Fill all the spaces to make the box as vibrant as possible – it'll show the person who is receiving the gift just how much they mean to you. Leave the design to firm up.

Be inspired by how the design on this box grows, then customise your art to suit you.

Totes ace tags

DohVinci

You will need:
Tracing paper, card, pencil, scissors, hole punch, ribbon, DohVinci Styler and Deco Pop tubes

How to make:

1. Use some tracing paper and the pencil to copy the gift tag templates on this page and retrace them onto card.

2. Cut out the tags and use a hole punch to make a hole at the top of each one, over the cross.

3. Thread a piece of ribbon through a hole, then make a loop and secure in a knot. Repeat for all the tags.

4. Write names on the tags, then adorn with DohVinci. Set aside to firm up.

Capture the World

What do you think the world will look like in 100 years?
Dream up a fantastic scene and sketch it here.
Then transform your ideas into DohVinci art.

Switch surfaces!
Create a
DohVinci design
for wood art.

"Creativity takes courage."
Henri Matisse – artist (1869–1954)

Snow Friend

DohVinci

What's your snow style? Photocopy, scan or cut out this page from the Annual and use your Styler to make a snow friend in spectacular 3D.

Mirror Me

Art is all about expressing yourself. Use this page to draw a self-portrait. It doesn't have to be an exact representation – think about shapes and colours that reflect your style. It's the ultimate selfie!

"Every good painter paints what he is."
Jackson Pollock - artist
(1912-1956)

School Swag

Leave boring behind and turn heads when you transform your school life with DohVinci decorations! What's your colour style? Show everybody who you are.

All you need is your DohVinci Styler, Deco Pop Tubes and your imagination. Remember to ask an adult before decorating anything with the DohVinci compound.

Colourful memo board for your locker.

All you need is your DohVinci Styler,
Deco Pop Tubes and your imagination.

Arty notebook

Sweet pencil holder.

Amazing Makes

Take pictures of all your design achievements and stick them in a collage on this album page. Snap a few selfies with your DohVinci Styler too!

Art-tastic Wish List

Biscuit jar

Check out these way-cool suggestions for your next art project. Note down your ideas here too! You never know when you'll get the urge to make, create and decorate in beautiful, keepable, giftable 3D....

Keepsake Box

Remember to ask an adult before you upcycle or decorate something from home.

You can display your designs immediately as the compound won't drip or run - but always handle your completed design with care.

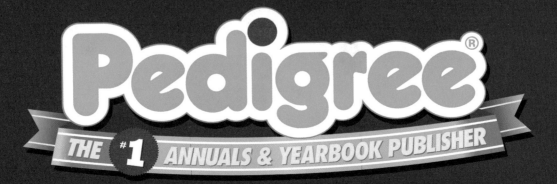